COMIC ART

by Ryan Gale

BrightPoint Press

San Diego, CA

BrightPoint Press

© 2022 BrightPoint Press
an imprint of ReferencePoint Press, Inc.
Printed in the United States

For more information, contact:
BrightPoint Press
PO Box 27779
San Diego, CA 92198
www.BrightPointPress.com

LIBRARY OF CONGRESS CATALOGING-IN-PUBLICATION DATA

Names: Gale, Ryan, author.
Title: Comic art / Ryan Gale.
Description: San Diego, CA : BrightPoint Press, [2022] | Series: Exploring art | Includes
    bibliographical references and index. | Audience: Grades 7-9
Identifiers: LCCN 2021007435 (print) | LCCN 2021007436 (eBook) | ISBN 9781678201203
    (hardcover) | ISBN 9781678201210 (eBook)
Subjects: LCSH: Comic books, strips, etc.--Juvenile literature.
Classification: LCC PN6710 .G26 2022 (print) | LCC PN6710 (eBook) | DDC 741.5/9--dc23
LC record available at https://lccn.loc.gov/2021007435
LC eBook record available at https://lccn.loc.gov/2021007436

CONTENTS

AT A GLANCE

- Comic art uses images and text to tell stories. This type of art includes comic strips, comic books, graphic novels, and webcomics. There is comic art for people of all ages.

- Newspaper cartoons grew into comic strips in the early 1800s.

- Swiss artist Rodolphe Töpffer made the first comic book in 1827.

- Superhero comic books became popular in the late 1930s and 1940s.

- Some people used to burn comic books. They thought comics were a bad influence on children.

- Some comic art is made by a single person. Some is made by several people working together.

- Some comic artists draw comics by hand. They use pencils and paper. Others draw using computer software. Some use both.

- Comic art has been used to promote awareness for social, racial, and health issues.

- Comic art has had a major influence on the entertainment industry. Comics have been turned into television shows, movies, and video games.

THE ART OF STORYTELLING

Sarah browsed the rows of comic art at her local bookstore. She saw a book of Garfield comic strips. Then she saw a graphic novel based on *The Hobbit*, a novel by J. R. R. Tolkien. She saw comic books about Spider-Man and Batman. Then Sarah found what she was looking for. It was the latest Wonder Woman comic.

Comics about superheroes are very popular.

Wonder Woman was her favorite superhero.

Sarah liked her super speed and strength.

She also liked that Wonder Woman was

smart and wise. New issues came out

every month.

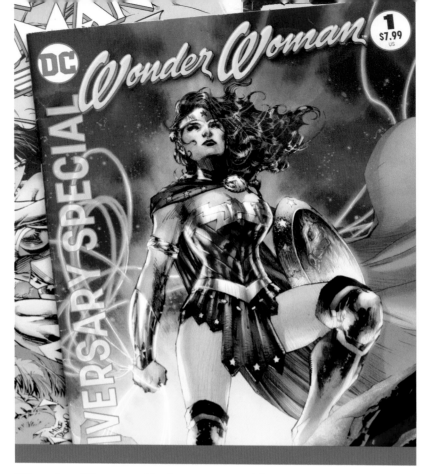

Wonder Woman first appeared in comic art in 1941. Since then, she's been a popular figure.

Sarah had collected Wonder Woman comics since she was young. She had also seen every Wonder Woman movie and television show. But Sarah liked the comic books best. She liked how the pictures and text worked together to tell stories. And she got to use her imagination. She used it to fill in the blank space between each picture. Sarah paid for the comic book and rushed home. She couldn't wait to read it.

GRAPHIC FICTION

Comic art is a mix of words and images. Artists combine them to tell stories. Comic art is sometimes called graphic fiction. People around the world enjoy comics. It is read by people of all ages.

The word *comic* means "funny." The art form is called comic art because many early examples were meant to be funny. But it evolved over more than 150 years. There are many different kinds of comic art today. Some comics are still funny, but some are serious. Others tell scary stories. Each work of comic art has a unique story to tell.

Comic art has affected our culture in many ways. Some of the most famous superheroes come from comics, such as Spider-Man, Batman, and Wonder Woman. Both children and adults sometimes dress up like their favorite comic characters. Comic art often crosses over into other art forms. These include television, movies, and video games. Early comic art had racism

Many people like to bring comic book characters to life by dressing up as them.

and **stereotypes**. But comic art was later used to fight racial injustice. Comics have also been used as teaching materials in schools. Many people see comic art as an amazing art form.

CHAPTER ONE

WHAT IS COMIC ART?

Comic art uses both text and images to tell stories. The images are usually drawings, but they can be photographs or digital art too. They can also be fine art such as paintings. Comic art uses images in unique ways. Each image is contained within a panel. The images are often combined with text. The text

Comic art can be very colorful.

may describe what happens. Or it may

be speech or thoughts. Text can also

represent sounds.

Each panel contains one part of a story.

The panels are arranged in **sequence**.

They are often laid out from left to right and

top to bottom. Panels usually have empty

spaces around them. These spaces are called gutters. The gutter represents the passage of time between each panel. It is up to readers to fill in these spaces using their imaginations.

TYPES OF COMIC ART

There are several types of comic art. Comic strips are short comics often seen

COMIC ART VS. CARTOON ART

Cartoon art also uses images to tell stories. But cartoon art is different from comic art. Cartoon art has only a single image. Comic art typically has two or more images in sequence. Like comic art, cartoon art is often found in newspapers and magazines.

in newspapers and magazines. Most have

two or more panels. Stories usually begin

and end in one strip.

Comic books are longer stories **bound**

in book format. They are often twenty-four

or thirty-two pages long. Stories may begin

and end in one book. Or they may be told over the course of several books. These are called **serial** comic books. Sometimes comic books that make up a series are bound together into one book. This is called a trade paperback. Comic books can also be collections of comic strips.

There are a few other types of comic art. Minicomics are homemade comic books. They are often printed on photocopiers or home printers. They are folded and bound by hand. Graphic novels are often more than one hundred pages long. They tell a complete story from start to finish.

People can find graphic novels at comic stores, bookstores, and libraries.

Webcomics are comic strips and books published online.

There are many **genres** of comic art. Comic strips are mostly humor. The superhero genre features powerful, heroic characters. Science fiction comics

may take place on other worlds or in the

future. Fantasy comics have elements

from the real world mixed with magic and

mythical creatures. Other genres include

MANGA

Manga is the Japanese word for "comic." Japanese manga has its own unique style. It is usually printed in black and white. Characters often have large eyes and small mouths. Their emotions are often highly exaggerated. Unlike comics made in most other countries, manga reads from the right side to the left side. This means the front cover is where the back cover would be in books from most other countries. Manga is made this way because the written Japanese language is read from the right side to the left side.

horror, drama, and mystery. Television shows and movies are sometimes turned into comics. These include *Star Wars, Star Trek*, and the *Terminator*. Comics have also been made from the works of classic authors, such as Edgar Allan Poe, Mark Twain, and H. G. Wells.

BUYING AND COLLECTING COMIC ART

Comic art can be found in many places. Sunday editions of newspapers usually have several pages of comic strips printed in color. Monday through Saturday editions may only have a few strips. They are usually printed in black and white.

Comic books are sold in bookstores and in comic shops. Some grocery stores and gas stations sell comic books as well. In addition, comic books and graphic novels are sold at comic conventions. People who like comic art gather at these events. Comic book and webcomic publishers sell comic art on their websites. New and old comics are also sold on online marketplaces.

Comic art was once seen as disposable. It was printed on cheap paper. The art didn't last long. The paper easily tore. It became yellow as it aged. The staples holding the pages together would rust.

Comic artists will sometimes go to comic conventions to show off their artwork.

Comic art was meant to be read a few times and then thrown away. But as interest in comic art grew in the 1970s, people began to collect it.

Many people still collect comic art. Some people purchase it as an investment. They buy it, wait for its value to increase, and then sell it for a profit. Some people go to great lengths to protect their comic art. They store it in plastic bags. This keeps it in good condition. Comic books are worth more if they are in good condition. Some collectors buy two copies of a comic book. They read one copy. The other copy gets stored in a safe place. Some people collect the original artwork used to make comic books. It is sold by art dealers and auction companies.

People from all over the world like to look at and collect comic art.

THE STIGMA OF COMIC ART

Stigma has surrounded comic art

for many years. Comic art sometimes

displays violence. Some people think it

People may be just as engaged reading comics as they would be reading books or watching movies.

can make readers act violently. In addition,

not everyone thinks comic art is serious

literature. They see it as less complex

than other art forms. "At school, the

encouragement was always to pick up the books with words and no images," recalled writer Carina Pereira.[1]

Some people believe comic art is only meant for children. Or they may believe that only uneducated people read it. These are stereotypes. People of all ages and backgrounds enjoy comic art. It is an exciting way to tell stories. Annabel Doyle is a comic artist. She said that comic art "brings together the visual impact of watching a movie with the quiet intimacy of reading a book."[2]

CHAPTER TWO

WHAT IS THE HISTORY OF COMIC ART?

C omic art evolved from political cartoons from the 1700s and early 1800s. These cartoons were printed in European newspapers. They had only a single image. Some included text. In June 1825, the first issue of the *Glasgow Looking Glass* was published. It was a magazine

Some museums have comic art exhibits.

filled with cartoons. Some were funny.

Others showed life in the city of Glasgow,

Scotland. The fourth issue featured a comic

strip called "History of a Coat." Some

historians consider it to be the first comic

strip ever made. The first daily comic strip

was called *A. Piker Clerk*. It was created by Clare Briggs in 1903. It ran in the *Chicago American* newspaper until June 7, 1904. Many other daily comic strips followed. By the 1930s, most newspapers in the United States had comic strips in them.

Swiss artist Rodolphe Töpffer is often credited with making the first comic book. In 1827, he wrote the *History of Mr. Vieux Bois*. It was a romantic comedy told using drawings. The book was first published in Switzerland in 1837. It was published in the United States five years later. The title was changed to *The Adventures of*

Mr. Obadiah Oldbuck. It was the first comic book published in the United States. Other artists in Europe began making comic books in the mid-1800s.

In the late 1800s and early 1900s, comic makers began compiling their old comic

RACISM IN COMICS

Early comic art had stereotypes of Black people, Asian people, and other ethnic groups. Images of minorities in early comic art were often racist. The artists exaggerated physical features. They made minority characters speak English poorly. They used traditions from different cultures as sources for jokes. All of these things were hurtful. Over time, the comic industry became more racially sensitive.

strips into books. One of the most popular books was *Comics Monthly.* It was first published in 1922. Another was *Famous Funnies.* It was first released in 1933. Then *New Fun Comics* was published in 1935 by National Allied Publications. It had all-new material rather than reprints of old material. National Allied Publications would later become one of the largest US comic book companies: DC Comics.

THE GOLDEN AGE OF COMICS

The comic industry changed forever in 1938. In that year, National Allied Publications came out with *Action Comics.*

DC Comics is known for superheroes such as Batman, Superman, and Wonder Woman.

It featured a new superhero called Superman. This started an era known as the Golden Age of comics.

During World War II (1939–1945), superhero comic books were popular with US soldiers. They featured superheroes

World War II was the deadliest war in history.

such as Captain America and Batman.

These heroes fought the nation's wartime

enemies in Europe and the South Pacific.

They inspired people. Comics also included

messages. The messages asked people in

the United States to help pay for the war.

Publishers tried to inspire children during this time. They made comics featuring the Young Allies and the Boy Commandos. They were teams of kids who fought the enemies of the United States. Many people lost interest in superhero comics after the war. They no longer needed inspiration. Comic companies made crime and horror comics instead.

Not everyone appreciated comic books during this time. Many comics were violent. Some showed women wearing little clothing. Book critic Sterling North believed comic books were a bad influence on children. In a 1940 article he wrote, "Parents and teachers throughout America must band together to break the 'comic' magazine."[3] Many people agreed with North. People around the country began collecting comic books and burning them. Sales dropped in the late 1940s.

The US government responded to the public outcry against comic books. The Senate held a hearing in April 1954. Senators wanted to know if comic books made kids misbehave. Dr. Fredric Wertham spoke at the hearing. He argued that comics taught children how to be criminals.

Some people in Maine worked together to collect and then destroy comic books.

But the senators were not convinced. They did not see a need for the government to get involved. They said the comic book industry should **regulate** itself.

THE SILVER AGE OF COMICS

As a result of the Senate hearing, several comic companies formed the Comics Magazine Association of America in October 1954. Its goal was to regulate the comic book industry. It did this by creating the Comics Code Authority (CCA). The CCA created a set of rules for comic content. It was called the Comics Code. The code banned nudity, drug use, and bad language. It said that comics could not be violent. It said that in stories, good always had to triumph over evil. Most publishers had their comics reviewed by the CCA.

Charles F. Murphy (right) worked for the Comics Magazine Association of America. He reviewed comics.

These comics received the CCA's stamp of approval on their covers. Many stores would not sell comics without the stamp. This marked the end of the Golden Age of comics and the start of a new era. It came to be known as the Silver Age of comics.

Comic companies returned to making superhero comics. Superheroes were decent and respectable. It was easy to make superhero stories that followed the Comics Code. But comics made under this code did not sell well. Many people did not find them interesting. Several comic companies went out of business as a result.

In the late 1960s, comic artists started making comic books independent of mainstream publishers. Their comics had content not allowed by the Comics Code. The artists published and sold the books themselves. Their work came to be known

Today, comics don't need a stamp of approval from the CCA.

as comix. The comix movement helped

reignite interest in comic books. In the

1970s and 1980s, many people stopped

seeing comics as bad influences. The CCA

began loosening its rules as a result.

THE MODERN AGE OF COMICS

The Modern Age of comics began in the 1980s and continues today. The 1980s and 1990s were dominated by the two biggest comic book companies: Marvel and DC. But several smaller companies also emerged, such as Dark Horse Comics, Caliber, and Pacific Comics. Comic companies created many new characters during this time. Marvel and DC reinvented old characters too. Graphic novels also became popular. They included some of the most famous modern examples of comic art, such as *Batman: The Dark Knight Returns*, *Watchmen*, and *Maus*.

The Modern Age of comics is sometimes called the Dark Age of comics. The CCA's influence weakened during the 1980s

---

MAUS

Some people say that *Maus* is the greatest graphic novel ever made. It was written by Art Spiegelman. It was published in 1986. *Maus* was a true story about Spiegelman's father. It described how he survived a German military death camp in World War II. The characters in *Maus* were animals such as cats and mice. The book helped people better understand a difficult period in history. In 1992, *Maus* became the first comic to win a Pulitzer Prize. The Pulitzer is the highest national award for literature.

and 1990s. Comic books became darker and more serious as a result. They also become more violent. The line between good and evil became less clearly defined. **Antiheroes**, such as Spawn, Venom, and Deadpool, became popular. Horror comics also made a comeback. Marvel abandoned the Comics Code in 2001. All other comics companies did this as well by the end of 2011. This gave comic companies more freedom to print what they wanted.

Webcomics became popular in the 1990s and 2000s. Digital comics were first shared over the internet in the mid-1980s.

People can enjoy comic art online.

In the 1990s, comic artists began making websites for their comics. Later, they began posting comic art on social media sites. The internet allows anyone to publish his or her comic art. It is cheaper than printing comics. And there is no limit to content and length.

CHAPTER THREE

HOW IS COMIC ART MADE TODAY?

P eople who make comic art are known as comic artists. They can draw comics by hand or use computers to make their art. Both techniques can also be used together. Some comic artists create only the images. Writers produce the text. Other comic artists do both.

Comic book artist Ben Bishop focuses on creating a page of comic art.

Comic artists use a variety of tools. They draw images using pencils, pens, brushes, and ink. Rulers are often used to draw straight lines. Comic artists use different kinds of paper. They may use inexpensive paper for doing rough sketches. Then they may use better-quality paper for the final drawings. Comic artists often work on special drawing tables. The table surfaces are slanted. This keeps the artists from having to bend forward. Some artists use light boxes. These are boxes with lights inside. The tops have clear surfaces. They help artists trace images onto paper.

Many comic artists draw using computers. Some use a mouse for drawing. Others use drawing tablets. Drawing tablets plug into computers. They let artists create hand-drawn images. The images are shown on the computer screens. Comic artists

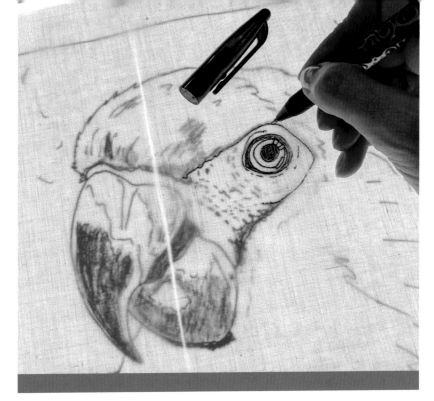

Artists of all kinds may use light boxes to help them create art.

use scanners for scanning hand-drawn art onto computers. They also use printers and photocopiers for printing artwork.

WRITING THE STORY

The first step in making comic art is coming up with an idea for a story or character.

A single person can come up with an original concept. Or two or more people may work together to develop one. The next step is turning the concept into a story line, or plot. Characters and settings are introduced. Conflict arises. The characters overcome the conflict. Comic strips often have simple plots. Comic books and graphic novels may have more complex ones.

Once a plot is developed, a script is written. The script outlines how many panels are on each page. It describes what happens in each panel. Speech and

PARTS OF A COMIC

Comics have many different features to help tell stories.

thoughts are included for each character.

Finished scripts are usually sent to editors

for review. The editors check for spelling and grammar mistakes.

Writing comics is unlike other forms of writing. According to comic writer Barry Lyga, "When you write a comic book, you need to think visually and then you need to communicate those visuals in such a way as to spark the artist's imagination to present them the way you see them."[4]

DRAWING AND COLORING

Once the script is done, the artwork can begin. The first step is creating thumbnails from the script. Thumbnails are simple sketches of each comic page. They are

Artists frequently practice drawing so they can make the best art possible.

used to work out the overall look of each

page. Thumbnails show where people and

objects should go. They show the angle of

each character and object. And they show

whether they are close or far away. Basic

landscapes are also included. Thumbnails

are often done on sketch pads using pencils or pens.

Thumbnails are used as guides for creating larger drawings. The drawings are done in pencil. This stage is called penciling. The drawings start out as simple outlines. Then details are added. Mistakes are fixed with an eraser. When finished, the drawings are traced onto better-quality paper. A light box is often used. The tracings are cleaner. They do not have eraser marks or other signs of mistakes. The lines are made bolder. The tracings will be used to make the finished artwork.

Comic book artists use their imaginations to bring stories to life.

When the final drawings are done, the

pencil lines are traced over in ink. This is

called inking. It is done using black pens or

with brushes dipped in black ink. Both may

be used in the same comic. Inking makes

the artwork more visible. Shadows are

added. Special effects, such as smudging

and splattering, are done as well.

   After inking comes lettering. This is when

text is added. Text is usually contained

TYPOGRAPHY

Typography is the art of arranging text, or
type, to make it easy to read and pleasing to
look at. It plays an important role in comic art.
There are many different styles of text. Some
styles convey emotions. Jagged text may show
anger. Crooked text may show confusion.
Some text styles are big and bold. They are
used to add emphasis to words. Color can
add further meaning to words. Red text can be
used to show anger. Blue text can be used to
show calmness.

in boxes, speech bubbles, and thought bubbles. Text also includes words that describe sounds. Text is often added using a computer. But it can also be printed onto labels. The labels are then attached to the artwork. Text can also be written by hand.

Coloring is the last stage in making comic art. Color makes the art more interesting. It can also help tell the story. "We set the tone and mood with color, we direct your eye across the page, and set up depth of field," explains comic colorist Dave McCaig.[5]

COMIC ART TODAY

Today, many artists make comics using computers. Some make comics from start to finish on computers. Others use these devices to do the inking, lettering, or coloring. Special design software is used to draw and paint. Mistakes are erased digitally.

Sometimes comic art is made by a single person. Other times, each step is done by a different artist. Stories are often written by professional writers. Pencilers do drawings, inkers do inking, letterers do lettering, and colorists do coloring.

Drawing tablets help people create art today.

Other people may be involved in printing,

marketing, and selling the comics.

A college degree is not required to be

a comic artist. But some comic writers

have degrees in English or creative

writing. Many artists get degrees in art, design, or illustration. Artists who make webcomics may have training in web design as well. Some art schools, such as the

PUBLISHING

Some comic artists publish their work through publishing companies. The companies print and distribute the comics for them. But the companies keep most of the profit. Getting comic art published this way can be difficult. Large comic companies create and publish their own comics. They do not usually accept submissions from other people. Some people publish their own comic art. This is called self-publishing. It can cost a lot of money. But artists who self-publish get to keep all of the profit.

With new technology, people are able to create amazing art from their homes.

Minneapolis College of Art and Design, offer

degrees in comic art. They teach specific

skills people need to become comic artists.

CHAPTER FOUR

WHAT IS THE CULTURAL IMPACT OF COMIC ART?

Comic art has had a major impact on our culture. Everything related to comics is considered part of comic culture. Comic art has affected the entertainment industry. Today, this includes television shows and movies. Comic characters

Many people today get a lot of enjoyment out of reading comic books.

have been featured in many cartoons and

live-action television shows. They have been

in many movies as well. This has helped the

comic industry reach people who may not

be interested in traditional comic art.

Some comic book characters have been made into action figures.

Comic art has impacted other forms

of entertainment as well. Many video and

board games have been made based on

comics. And comic characters have been

featured on merchandise. This includes

toys, clothing, school supplies, and greeting cards. People have also written books that feature comic art and artists. *The Amazing Adventures of Kavalier & Clay* is a book about two fictional comic book artists. It was written by Michael Chabon and was

FREE COMIC BOOK DAY

Free Comic Book Day (FCBD) is held every year on the first Saturday in May. The first FCBD was held in 2002. It is a day to celebrate comics. On this day, some comic book shops give away free comic books to visitors. Shops around the world participate. Some turn FCBD into community events. They host costume contests, book signings, and other activities.

published in 2000. It won a Pulitzer Prize for fiction.

BREAKING BARRIERS

Comic art has helped break down social and racial barriers. Most early comic art had only white, male lead characters. Over time, female, Native American, Asian, and Black characters appeared. In 2013, Marvel introduced a Muslim superhero named Ms. Marvel. Comics have also featured lesbian, gay, bisexual, transgender, and queer or questioning (LGBTQ) characters. They also include characters living with disabilities.

The comic industry has become more diverse as well. The numbers of female and Black comic artists have increased. Some have started their own companies that showcase Black and female characters.

STAN LEE

Stan Lee was a comic book writer and publisher. He had a major impact on the comic industry. Lee worked for Marvel Comics in the 1960s. He helped create many memorable characters, such as Spider-Man, Hulk, and Black Panther. Later, he was put in charge of content as the company's editorial director. He helped Marvel become a multimedia empire by expanding into television and movies. Lee was also the public face of Marvel. He often made appearances at comic book conventions. He also appeared on television shows and in movies. Lee passed away in 2018 at age 95.

The companies include Milestone Media and Hex Comix.

Comic art can raise awareness for many issues. These include racism and drug abuse. The Center for Cartoon Studies published a comic book to help young people deal with mental health issues. In 2020, comic publisher Graphic Medicine released a series of webcomics. The comics taught people about COVID-19. This was a disease that spread across the world beginning in late 2019. Many people died.

Comic art can be used as a teaching tool in classrooms. Comics are being used to

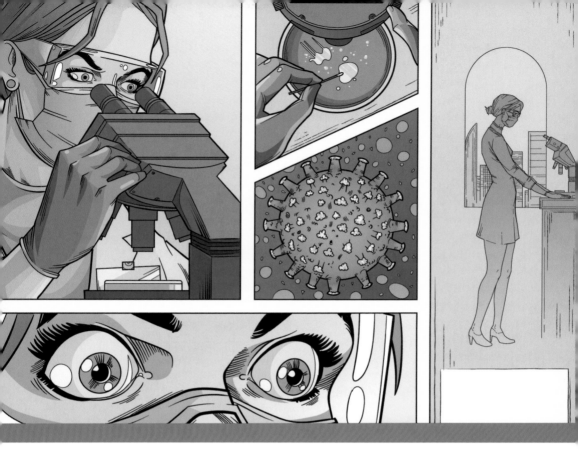

Some people have created comic art that shows researchers studying diseases.

teach subjects such as history and civics.

Tim Smyth is a high school history teacher.

He uses comic books in his classroom. He

says, "Comics serve as a time capsule for

society and my students are encouraged to

look at changes over time and analyze what they see."[6] Comics are also used to help struggling readers. The images can help them understand the meanings of words. In addition, comics are used to encourage reluctant readers. According to writer Jen Thames, "Comics break through one of the most important reading barriers with kids, and that is getting them interested in reading in the first place."[7]

FANDOM

People across the world are fans of comic art. They belong to one of many fan cultures, or fandoms. A fandom is a

Comic fans can find a wide variety of comic books at conventions.

large community of people with a shared

interest. Each year, members of the comic

art fandom get together. They gather at

comic book conventions. They come to

enjoy comics together. The San Diego Comic-Con is the world's largest comic convention. More than 135,000 people attended in 2019. The convention brings comic artists, celebrities, and fans together. Major news outlets often cover the event.

Many people go to comic conventions dressed as their favorite comic characters. This is called costume play, or cosplay. Some people make their own costumes. Other people buy them. Some people spend thousands of dollars on their costumes. People also dress up as comic characters for Halloween.

The San Diego Comic-Con has panels of people who work in the comic book industry.

Some people go all out when dressing as their favorite characters.

Superhero costumes are often sold in stores. Costumes are a big part of the comic fandom.

Comic art continues to evolve. It remains an important part of US culture. There is an endless number of tales to be told. Comic art will tell stories long into the future.

GLOSSARY

antiheroes

main characters who lack typical heroic qualities

bound

secured to a cover by cord, tape, or glue

genres

categories of art or literature having particular forms, content, or techniques

literature

writings that are viewed as important and having a lasting impact

regulate

to control or direct by rules

sequence

the following of one thing after another in order

serial

appearing in parts at regular intervals

stereotypes

assumptions that all members of a group of people share the same qualities

stigma

signifying that something is shameful

SOURCE NOTES

CHAPTER ONE: WHAT IS COMIC ART?

1. Carina Pereira, "The Value and Educational Benefit of Reading Comics," *Book Riot*, September 16, 2019. https://bookriot.com.

2. Annabel Doyle, "Newbies' Guide to Comic Art," *Adobe*, July 17, 2018. https://blog.adobe.com.

CHAPTER TWO: WHAT IS THE HISTORY OF COMIC ART?

3. Sterling North, "A National Disgrace and a Challenge to American Patents," *Taylor & Francis Online*, September 12, 2013. www.tandfonline.com.

CHAPTER THREE: HOW IS COMIC ART MADE TODAY?

4. Barry Lyga, "How to Write Comic Books," *Barry Lyga*, n.d. https://barrylyga.com.

5. Quoted in Arune Singh, "Dave McCaig Talks 'Superman: Birthright,'" *CBR*, August 15, 2003. www.cbr.com.

CHAPTER FOUR: WHAT IS THE CULTURAL IMPACT OF COMIC ART?

6. Tim Smyth, "How I Use Comic Books As a Learning Tool in My Social Studies Classroom," *PBS*, March 29, 2016. www.pbs.org.

7. Jen Thames, "Comic Books Help Students Learn to Read and Improves Comprehension," *Learn to Read Comics*, April 12, 2013. https://learntoreadcomics.org.

FOR FURTHER RESEARCH

BOOKS

Stuart A. Kallen, *The Art of Comics*. San Diego, CA: ReferencePoint Press, 2020.

W. L. Kitts, *Careers in Animation and Comics*. San Diego, CA: ReferencePoint Press, 2020.

Christa Schneider, *Make It Yourself! Comics & Graphic Novels*. Minneapolis, MN: Abdo, 2018.

INTERNET SOURCES

Tim DeForest, "DC Comics," *Britannica*, April 2, 2020. www.britannica.com.

Ernie Estrella, "The 25 Greatest Comic Book Artists from the Last 25 Years," *Syfy*, August 23, 2019. www.syfy.com.

"Who Invented Comic Books?" *Wonderopolis*, n.d. www.wonderopolis.org.

WEBSITES

DC Comics
www.dccomics.com

DC Comics is the official site for DC's comic books, movies, television shows, and games.

Free Comic Book Day
www.freecomicbookday.com

Free Comic Book Day provides information on the annual Free Comic Book Day event held every year on the first Saturday in May.

Making Comics
www.makingcomics.com

Making Comics provides free learning materials on how to create and publish comic art.

INDEX

IMAGE CREDITS

ABOUT THE AUTHOR

Ryan Gale is a Minnesota-based artist and writer. He enjoys visiting his local comic shop.